Is Your Belief Enough?

Pastor Lindsay McMurtry

ISBN 979-8-89112-162-1 (Paperback)
ISBN 979-8-89112-163-8 (Digital)

Copyright © 2024 Pastor Lindsay McMurtry
All rights reserved
First Edition

Cover Art by Frankie McMurtry

All rights reserved. No part of this publication may be reproduced, distributed, or transmitted in any form or by any means, including photocopying, recording, or other electronic or mechanical methods without the prior written permission of the publisher. For permission requests, solicit the publisher via the address below.

Covenant Books
11661 Hwy 707
Murrells Inlet, SC 29576
www.covenantbooks.com

God has always been faithful to me! However, for a long time, I lived with just my belief, and I thought it was enough. I gave nothing more to God other than recognition. Through some traumatic events in my life, God spoke to me often, asking
"Is it enough?"
So now I am asking you—
Is your belief enough?

—Pastor Lindsay McMurtry

1
DAY

So often I hear the utterance of "Thank God" when something amazing happens—I'm talking truly amazing! Like when someone goes into remission from cancer, you will hear people say, "Praise the Lord!" When asked if they believe in Jesus, the answer is often yes. But I am finding more and more, that is where it ends. Much like Jesus is an elf on a shelf, they get Him out of the closet for special, stressful, overwhelming, or joyous events, but when the hype of that event simmers down, they put Him right back in the closet. You don't even let Him stay until the end of the party, so to speak. And while I am thankful and grateful for your belief, I often wonder, "Is your belief enough?"

I am often in awe when a celebrity or a popular singer gets up on stage and gives God the glory! When they start their speech with "I couldn't have done this without the Lord's help!" While this is 1,000 percent true! It just blows my mind that they would have the guts to say that on a public platform! Especially in the world we live in today! But I wonder if that's where it ends. Is their belief enough?

When an athlete points to the sky on their way out to the court or field, I've always wanted to think that it is their shout-out to God, whether it's to say "thank you," "please protect me," or to ask for a blessing on their abilities. But oftentimes, you will hear them say later that their mom, dad, or maybe even grandparents are watching out for them. Statements like that make me wonder: If you believe that your loved ones are in heaven, wouldn't that also mean that you believe in God? So then, why aren't you giving credit to the only Holy One? That is where the credit is due!

Where it breaks down for me is in John 14:6: "Jesus told him, I am the way, the truth and the life. No one can come to the Father except through me." So it would be my understanding that if you have the foundation of belief, you would want to and desire to know more about Jesus Christ and His Father, God. Would it be enough if we made no other attempts to know God? Or never get to know Jesus on a deeper level? If we just continue to live the same life and change nothing, would it be enough to get into Heaven?

These are the hard questions we will look at over the next thirty days. I want us to think about and maybe reassess some things in our lives. Take time to listen to what God is telling us. Only God can change you! But you have to want God!

2
DAY

In your dreams, what do you envision heaven being like? Do you ever wonder? Do you think it's going to be magnificent? Something beyond our imagination? I always think of my dad sitting in his canoe with his former dogs on the stillest water, and it's just peaceful. My dad loved the wilderness and everything about God's creation.

Which makes me wonder how some people either simply don't believe or make comments such as "Heaven can't handle me" or "Heaven is going to be so boring, just singing and dancing all day long." For one thing, each individual is a creation of God Almighty! He wouldn't have created you if heaven couldn't handle you! And I personally cannot wait to sing and dance in all His Glory! But for those of you who think that that is all that happens in heaven, y'all are mistaken! We will each have jobs to do. Mansions to maintain, and lots of food to consume! (And never have to worry about calories again)!

To the ones who claim that the alternative is a better option…

Let me ask you this. Would you ever build a bonfire, feed it for hours, get it superhot with the flames roaring, and then go lie down on it? Take a nap on it? Would you let your kids jump on it? I don't know about you, but I don't even like my showers to be too hot! Let alone watching my skin literally melt off my body! Even if you just fell into the fire and got right out, you would have months and months of agonizing treatments and healing to go through. I am going to guess that the majority of you are not willing to lie down and take a nap in a firepit. Then can you please tell me WHY you would choose to be engulfed in a lake of fire for ALL of eternity? Please explain this phenomenon to me! Because I don't understand it. God says, "Worship me, my Son, and the Holy Spirit," and you say, "No—I want to burn alive for eternity"?

I have heard some people say that hell is temporary. If you don't make it to heaven, then you just go to hell for a little while until you pay off whatever you need to pay off. I'm going to tell you that twisting the truth of God's words to suit your own personal needs and desires has never worked for anyone.

Hebrews 13:8 says, "Jesus Christ is the same yesterday, today and forever." And Malachi 3:6 says, "I am the Lord, and I do not change…"

He has made it very clear that He remains the same then, now, and forever. So I need you to ask yourself: Why do you think Jesus would bend the rules just for you? If you have been believing lies or creating your own lies to justify things in your life, it's time for you to get on your knees and start begging for forgiveness. Telling God a handful of "Yeah buts" later on is not going to help you. Don't leave the truth sitting on a shelf.

3

DAY

Today's content is not suitable for children. It's really not suitable for anyone, but it is the truth. The truth can be scary, and this is the simple reality.

I often hear people say, "If God loves us so much, and He created us, and we are His sons and daughters, and He is the GOD OF MERCY, then there is no way He would send one of His children to hell!" Some take it even further and say that they don't believe in hell, also for the reasons listed above. But the truth is, God sent His Son, Jesus Christ, to die on the cross for our sins! So that we might avoid hell. Folks, this is real. This isn't about whether or not you believe in hell. Because if you're still reading along, that means that you have confessed that you believe in God. You are searching for more answers about prayer, about Jesus Christ, and about the Bible. If you have confessed these things, then you know hell is real. The Bible warns us of what hell is. It was created for Satan, the angels who fell with him, and anyone who wants to mock God and not live a life dedicated to Him. (This may be a long one, folks; there is a lot to go over, and with a subject this sensitive, I don't want to leave any holes.)

We can start with Revelations 21:8: "But cowards, unbelievers, the corrupt, murderers and immoral, those who practice witchcraft, idol worshipers, and the liars, their fate is in the fiery lake of burning sulfur. This is the second death."

Folks, it starts with cowardice! That's as simple as denying God and being a coward when you speak the name of Jesus. Matthew 10:33 says, "But everyone who denies me here on Earth, I will also deny before my Father in Heaven." This means you can live a good life. You can be a good person! You can do all the right things! But if you don't believe (for the second thing on the list is simply an unbeliever) and you deny Jesus Christ, your fate lies within the lake of burning sulfur. Notice! Nowhere does that say that hell is a party! Or that it is drunken stupidity with whatever you say goes! If you think that you're choosing an eternity of downright partying, then you have been eating all the lies the enemy is feeding you.

Let's talk about eternity for a moment! I'm not even sure how to properly explain forever. Our physical lives here on earth will seem like a blink of the eye compared to eternity. Our struggles, our pain, and our earthly bodies are temporary. We have to temporarily say "no" to sin. We have to temporarily say "no" to our deepest temptations. We have to TEMPORARILY struggle with the things of this world that we want but that are not for us. God doesn't want us to suffer, but HE does want us to live holy lives! And strive to be like Jesus more and more every day! Don't you think that this temporary struggle is worth an eternity with God? In heaven, these struggles will be no more. There will be NO MORE PAIN! NO MORE SORROW! It sounds a lot better than the fiery, burning lake of sulfur! Since we chose Jesus, we will get to sing and dance His praises on the streets of gold! We will get to hug and laugh with the ones who went before us! How cool would it be to have dinner with Moses? Or Noah?

Romans 6:23 says, "For the wages of sin is death, but the free gift of God is eternal life through Christ Jesus our Lord." God wants the best for us. He wants us for His kingdom! Our earthly desires make it difficult! But our earthly desires are only temporary! Remember that! Our earthly lives are short and temporary!

1 John 2:25 says, "And in the fellowship we enjoy the eternal life He promised us!"

4
DAY

Do you believe in God Almighty? Do you believe that there is a being that took time to intricately design what we call earth? Do you believe that there is a being that knew thousands of years ago that you would walk the earth at this specific time in history? Do you believe that there is a being that created so many different kinds of animals, plants, and trees? Do you believe that the same being placed every single hair on your head carefully? Do you believe God has always been here? He was the first—the one and only!

I think it is natural to ask, "Where did He come from?" I believe that is part of the wonder. We will know when we get to our forever home with Him.

Revelations 22:13 says, "I am the Alpha and the Omega, the First and the Last, the Beginning and the End."

God created the heavens! God created the earth! I wonder if God was ever lonely? Maybe that is why He created the earth? Maybe that is why He created humans! I don't believe that God would ever want to be alone again. For me personally, I cannot imagine how lonely He must have been all that time! All the time before He came up with the idea of the earth. Planning the earth, most likely, eased some of that loneliness by keeping Him busy. Aside from severe loneliness, God loves us beyond our comprehension!

I know it's hard to believe in something you've never seen before. However, there is no way you can tell me that you have never felt Him, felt His presence, or felt Him speak gently to you. You may have pushed it aside and given some other excuse for it, but I have felt my blood run cold for no apparent reason. I have also felt it run hot. I have felt peace rush over me like a flood in times when there was no way I was going to calm down. That is usually when He is trying hard to get my attention! How hard does He have to try to get your attention?

Can you really tell me that it is easier for you to believe that there is nothing after we take our last breath as humans? That it is easier to believe that we will never again see our loved ones who have gone before us? For me, that is harder to believe. I could never imagine that I would never see my dad again, my grandma, or my grandpa. That, to me, is unfathomable!

I have heard some people say that they don't know what they believe. The hard facts are that if you don't believe in something, then that must mean you believe in something else. If you do not believe in God, then you are putting your faith and belief in something else. If you can't figure out what that is, then you are believing solely in yourself. And that, my friends, is a dangerous thing to do.

Luke 20:38 says, "So He is the God of the living, not the dead, for that are all alive to Him."

Revelations 21:4 says, "He will wipe every tear from their eyes, and there will be no more death or sorrow or crying from pain. All these things are gone forever."

The only tears that will be shed in heaven will be tears of joy. Tears from our loved ones who have patiently waited for us. The ones who have been praying that we find salvation! So that we can have that glorious reunion!

For those who deny the Lord until their last breath, they will suffer spiritual and physical death. They will suffer that death for eternity. Death equals hell. There will be no joyous reunions. If you do see a loved one among the sufferers, there will be no joy. There will be shame—that they fell for all the lies and that they never gave the Lord a chance. There will be plenty of tears. Tears that are shed out of anguish and turmoil, which I think is worse than sorrow.

Matthew 25:41 says, "Then the King will turn to those on the left and say, 'away with you, you cursed ones, into the eternal fire prepared for the devil and his demons.'"

Your beliefs are your choice! You have free will! But like all choices…There are consequences for the bad ones and rewards for the good ones!

5
DAY

I hope you have taken the time to really think about some of the questions asked in the first couple of days. Did any of them hit harder than the others? Did you stop to pray for any of them? Did some feelings get stirred up that you didn't know you had? Let's start taking a deeper look at your faith. What do you want to do with your beliefs? Do you want to learn more? Do you talk to God daily? Do you read your Bible to learn more about Him? When do you pray? Do you pray every day for your everyday problems? Do you make sure to thank Him for your victories? Or do you only cry out to Him when nothing seems to be going right and you feel like you have to bring out the bargaining chips?

The Bible says in Philippians 4:6–7, "Don't worry about anything; instead, pray about everything. Tell God what you need, and thank Him for all He has done. Then you will experience God's peace, which exceeds anything we can understand. His peace will guard your hearts and minds as you live in Christ Jesus."

Did you see how that started? Read it again: "Don't worry about anything." God doesn't want to bargain with you! He wants you to trust Him! He wants you to give Him your problems! That means you have to give up your control over things!

It then continues with "instead, pray about everything." God wants to be involved in every area of your life! Not just the AWESOME parts! Or the SUPER UGLY parts! But every part! It then says, "Tell God what you need, and thank Him for what He's done." We must remember to thank God! Just as we thank our friends and family for the gifts they have given us. When God answers our prayers, those are His gifts to us.

God also knows our hearts. He hears our every thought and every word. He's waiting for us to pour our hearts out to Him. That is why it says, "Tell God what you need."

Have you ever experienced God's peace? That indescribable, absolutely amazing feeling of calmness when the world seems to fall apart around you—those moments when you feel like you are in limbo, waiting for test results, waiting for a diagnosis, or waiting to see if a specific treatment is going to work. In those moments, when God brings His peace upon you, there is no denying that it is God. Will you, or can you, give God control over the situation? Will you allow God to give you that peace? God gave each one of us free will (which we will discuss later), but that means that in our free will, we have to choose God in order to receive what God has in store for us.

6
DAY

How much stock do you put in the Bible? Do you believe the Bible to be God's Word? Think about why or why not. Do you watch the news and believe it to be true? Do you watch documentaries? Do you believe they are true? What about the textbooks at school? What about the fundamentals—math and science? When you were in school, did you believe what you were being taught?

Then we have the Bible, which has stood the test of time. It has survived thousands of years. Don't you think there is a reason for that? Don't you think there is a reason you can find a Bible in every hotel room? Or in airport lounges? In every store's book department? How could we deny its validity?

The Bible says in 2 Timothy 3:16–17, "All scripture is inspired by God and is useful to teach us what is true and to make us realize what is wrong in our lives. It corrects us when we are wrong and teaches us to do what is right. God uses it to prepare and equip His people to do every good work."

Take a moment to think about those words. Maybe reread that verse a couple of times. Because there are a few things that stand out to me. For one, the verse starts by saying, "All scripture is inspired by God." Did you get that keyword—INSPIRED? There is a reason why the Bible has different books inside of it, all with different names—Matthew, Mark, Luke, John, etc. These books were written by different people to record their particular accounts of Jesus's life. They wrote about their encounters with God! Just as the news is inspired by what is going on in the world today, it is written from the perspective of the person witnessing it. Had I been present, my account may have differed slightly. Same for you, but in reality, we would have all witnessed the same thing.

I am asking you to try to read your Bible. Not only is it a great way to lift your spirits, but you will also be learning more about Jesus Christ, the one you believe in! You will learn more about the heart of God! It will give time for the Holy Spirit to speak to you on a deeper level! He will start to tell you if your belief is enough! He will start to tell you about the areas in your life in which you need to ask for forgiveness and to start praying for God to help change those areas, which we will talk more about later. The waterfall effect from reading your Bible for inspiration and direction is intimate and beautiful! Just start reading and see what happens!

7
DAY

Listen, folks, I used to be one of those people who said, "I don't need to go to church to believe in God." I used that line for a long time! But along with that line were the fingers pointing at me and "Christians" alike calling me a hypocrite! Why? Because there was nothing in my life that would lead anyone to believe that I was a Christian. I hung out at bars and swore like a sailor! I didn't want or need to answer to anyone! Since I grew up in the church, I just pretended like I had an invisible seal on my life. Like no matter what I did, I was going to go to heaven! While I know that God never left my side during that time, He was also begging me to come back to His kingdom and to once again become a child of God.

A big part of returning to church is that there is accountability there, support from God-loving friends, and the family of God to help lift you up.

It says in Revelations 3:15–17,

> I know all things you do, that you are neither hot or cold. I wish that you were one or the other! But since you are like lukewarm water, neither hot or cold, I will spit you out of my mouth! You say "I am rich. I have everything I want. I don't need anything!" And you don't realize that you are wretched miserable and poor and blind and naked.

God wants you to be all in or all out! He's unwilling to put up with a one-foot-in and one-foot-out commitment. He will give you warnings! And numerous chances to correct your choices! But He also wants an honest answer.

No matter how content you may feel in life—maybe you have a great job, a great salary, or a great family, everything is just great—there will always be a void you feel that you just can't explain. It will always feel like something is missing. You need to be all-in on Jesus! Let Jesus fill you up! Jesus will always be the answer to the void you feel.

Surrounding yourself with other Christ followers helps by encouraging and lifting each other up. Hebrews 10:25 says, "And let us not neglect our meeting together, as some people do, but encourage one another, especially now that the day of His return is drawing near."

It is not possible to live life as you want and on your terms and also be a Christ follower. It is time for you to decide! It's crazy how this one decision then makes the decision for you on many other questions! This decision will also determine where you spend eternity. It will help you decide if the relationship you are in is God-approved or if things need to change. It will decide what your activities will be for the following weekend. But it will also determine if you will live a fruitful, fulfilled life.

8
DAY

Did you know that God, Jesus, and the Holy Spirit, while they each act on their own and work in their own ways, are also all tied together as one? It is sad to say that the Holy Spirit has received the short end of the stick and has been put on the back burner. Some churches don't talk about Him at all. Being a part of the movement of the Holy Spirit is incredible. There is no way to describe the absolute beauty of it. Which is why it baffles me that He is pushed aside!

Have you ever heard of the Holy Spirit? What have you been taught about the Holy Spirit? First Corinthians 6:19–20, "Don't you realize that your body is the temple of the Holy Spirit, who lives in you and was given to you by God? You do not belong to yourself. For God bought you with a high price (His Son dying on the cross) So you must Honor God with your body."

So get this. There are people walking around with the Holy Spirit hanging out inside of them. He's probably banging around like a starving prisoner because He isn't being used! He isn't being acknowledged. His host has no desire to get to know Him or speak to Him because no one has told him about Him. It's time to start treating the Holy Spirit as an equal to God because He is a piece of God, the same as Jesus. We are capable of worshiping each one of them on a level playing field!

Matthew 28:19 says, "Therefore, go and make disciples of all the nations, baptizing them in the name of the Father, and the Son and the Holy Spirit."

All three! We bless people in the name of the Father, the Son, and the Holy Spirit, so why don't we speak of the Holy Spirit? The Holy Spirit is directly connected with the speaking of tongues, as in Acts 2:3–4, "Then what looked like flames or tongues of fire appeared and settled on each of them. And everyone present was filled with the Holy Spirit and began speaking in other languages, as the Holy Spirit gave them this ability."

Is this society afraid of the supernatural? Even when it comes from our Heavenly Father? But we look to rocks and stones for healing. We look at astronomy to tell us who we get along with. I'm a Virgo who married a Scorpio. So tell me how all that works. We search for all these strange ideas instead of trusting our Creator for everything He has to offer. Did you know that the Holy Spirit does more than just hand out foreign languages that we don't understand?

The Holy Spirit does so much more. Galatians 5:22–23 says, "But the Holy Spirit produces this kind of fruit in our lives; love, joy, peace, patience, kindness, goodness, faithfulness, gentleness, and self-control."

There is no law against these things! I don't know about you, but I sure could use all of those things—peace and self-control! The Holy Spirit has so much to offer! So why are we setting Him aside? Why are we not embracing all He has to offer?

The Bible gives this warning:

> So I tell you, every sin and blasphemy can be forgiven-except blasphemy against the Holy Spirit, which will never be forgiven. Anyone who speaks against the Son of man can be forgiven, but anyone who speaks against the Holy Spirit will never be forgiven either in this world or in the world to come. (Matthew 12:31–32)

It is time to embrace the Holy Spirit! And see what He has to offer you!

9
DAY

So this verse had me baffled for some time. I prayed a lot about it and sought counsel. I did not want to say something that was wrong. Matthew 12:31–33 says,

> So I tell you, every sin and blasphemy can be forgiven—except blasphemy against the Holy Spirit, which will never be forgiven. Anyone who speaks against the Son of Man can be forgiven, but anyone who speaks against the Holy Spirit will never be forgiven, either in this world or in the world to come.

(Blasphemy: The act or offense of speaking sacrilegiously about God; profane talk.)

This absolutely threw me for a loop! I had never heard that there was anything that you could not be forgiven for!

So let's back up a little bit. Matthew 6:14 says, "If you forgive those who sin against you, your Heavenly Father will forgive you." And then in Luke 6:37, it says, "Do not judge others, and you will not be judged. Do not condemn others, or it will all come back against you. Forgive others, and you will be forgiven."

And now it's saying that if I speak ill of the Holy Spirit, I will never be forgiven of that offense for all of eternity?

But Jesus FORGAVE the men who betrayed Him! He FORGAVE those who beat Him to a pulp, nailed Him to the cross, and left Him there to die! Jesus said, "Father, forgive them for they don't know what they are doing" (Luke 23:24).

Jesus was thoroughly beaten for each one of us. He did this to cover each one of our sins, down to what some of us feel are the lowest of lows. So Jesus will forgive murderers? Rapists? Child abusers?

Here's how it has been broken down for me: It says in Matthew 10:33, "But everyone who denies me here on earth, I will also deny before my Father in Heaven." Well, it would be impossible to deny Jesus before you ever knew Him, right?

The Holy Spirit is the one who convicts us of our sins. He's the one who tells us that we need to fix, apologize, or change something about ourselves. However, that is not possible to do before knowing Him and having a relationship with Him. Blasphemy comes in when you have struck up that relationship with Him. When you have welcomed Him into your life and then refuse to listen to Him, refuse to give Him credit for His work, or give something else credit for His work. If you aren't going to listen to Him, then why would He continue to talk to you? If the Holy Spirit cannot convict you of your sins, then how can you repent? How can Jesus forgive you?

I know this is a lot. Pray!

10
DAY

There are so many different areas of sin. There may be a variety of ways to look at those differences. I believe that the word itself—SIN—has become jaded. It has taken on various meanings and different looks over the past couple of years. I'm not sure if it is because people simply don't care anymore, or perhaps it is because people are so wrapped up in their own lives and trying to find what makes them happy here on this earth. They are so busy that they lose sight of what sin actually is.

Do you believe that we are all sinners? Do you believe that is why Jesus had to die on the cross? To save us from ourselves!

When I was younger, we had all this jewelry and clothing with the letters WWJD on them. Those letters stood for What Would Jesus Do? It was a reminder of who we belonged to.

Now all I see is "What would make you HAPPY? You need to find your inner peace. Look at your inner beast! Search yourself. You are stronger than you believe." There are T-shirts and a lot of home decor items that are now focused on looking at your own self for personal strength and uplifting. Now I know I can search my heart all day long, but I will never find enough strength or courage to do anything without the direction of my Lord and Savior!

The Lord directed me to create this thirty-day devotional! I rely on the Lord to direct the words that I write. I pray daily for guidance and direction. I pray that everything I write is in accordance with His Word! I pray that these words reach the people that they are meant to reach. Let me tell you, when I think I have a better idea and try to go in a different direction, or I think of a different topic that would be better next, He is quick to give me writer's block or block the ability to find the Scripture that I need to support the subject I want to work on. But then He slowly guides me back to what He wants. This devotional is not about me. This devotional belongs to God, His Son, Jesus Christ, and the Holy Spirit.

Jeremiah 10:23–24 says this: "I know Lord, that our lives are not our own. We are not able to plan our own course. So correct me Lord, but please be gentle. Do not correct me in anger, for I would die."

And that is what He does! Just as we redirect a two-year-old's attention to something else. God just slowly moves our attention to something that is more inclusive of Him.

Because God created us, we are to worship Him. We are to tell the world about Him. We are not to worship ourselves. People spend billions a year on self-help books. These books will tell you what to say to yourself in the mirror in the morning to encourage yourself to have the best day possible.

Save your money. Pray. Follow God's lead. Start worshipping Him first. Stop worshiping His creation! This includes yourself, other people, nature, etc.

For 1 Corinthians 6:19–20 says, "Don't you realize that your body is the temple of the Holy Spirit, who lives in you and was given to you by God? You don't belong to yourself, for God bought you with a high price. So, you must honor God with your body."

11
DAY

There is so much controversy these days over what sin is. There are arms being thrown up in the air everywhere, saying, "This is how God made me." God doesn't make mistakes! While both of those statements are true, it is also true that we are all sinners! We are all in desperate need of Jesus! I can honestly say that I am a sinner saved by God's grace and mercy! That doesn't mean I can continue in my sins. It means I too am human, and God is working on me. There are things that I do and habits that I have that I would have never known were sins, but God is slowly showing them to me!

But no worries! I am not going to sit here and tell you what your sins are. I am not going to try to tell you that anyone's lifestyle is sinful. Because at the end of the day, that is between you and the Lord! He is the one and only one who is capable of judging us in the end, and His judgment is the only one that will ever matter. I will, however, ask you to pray! Seek God! Ask Him to reveal your sins to you. When He reveals your sins, you will know what you need to work on. With God on your side, you will work together, and He will help you overcome your sins, which He has placed before you. Notice that I said WITH God! This is not something you can do on your own!

> So put to death the sinful, earthly things lurking within you. Have nothing to do with sexual immortality, impurity, lust and evil desires. Don't be greedy, for a greedy person is an idolator, worshipping the things of this world. Because

> of these sins, the anger of God is coming. You used to do these things when your life was still a part of this world. But now is the time to get rid of anger, rage, malicious behavior, slander, and dirty language. Don't lie to each other, for you have stripped off your old sinful nature and all its wicked deeds. Put on your new nature, and be renewed as you learn to know your creator and become like Him. (Colossians 3:5–10)

It's time to let God renew you. I know I would never want to see the anger of God!

> When you follow the desires of your sinful nature, the results are very clear: sexual immortality, impurity lustful pleasures, idolatry, sorcery, hostility, quarrelling, jealousy, outbursts of anger, selfish ambition, dissension, division, envy, drunkenness, wild parties, and other sins like these. Let me tell you again, as I have before, that anyone living that sort of life will not inherit the Kingdom of God. (Galatians 5:19–21)

Are you willing to deny your inheritance to the kingdom of God for those things that have no benefit to your life? Spend time asking God to reveal Himself to you, and His desires for you. Take the time to listen to Him.

DAY 12

Do you think there are different levels of sin? Do you think some sins are worse than others? Like in the justice system, there are different sentences for different things. A murderer will get a longer sentence than a shoplifter. Do you think God thinks the same way?

Galatians 5:19–21 says,

> When you follow the desires of your sinful nature the results are very clear: sexual immorality, impurity, lustful pleasures, idolatry, sorcery, hostility, quarrelling, jealousy, outbursts of anger, selfish ambition, dissension, division, envy, drunkenness, wild parties, and other sins like these. Let me tell you again, as I have before, that anyone living that sort of life will not inherit the Kingdom of God.

Look at that list! Did you notice something? Everything on that list is not even punishable by man's law! These are the things that many of us try to tell ourselves are okay. That there is nothing wrong with us for being a part of these things.

1 John 1:8–10 says,

> If we claim we have no sin, we are only fooling ourselves, and not living in the truth. but if we confess our sins to Him, He is faithful and

just to forgive us our sins and to cleanse us from all wickedness. If we claim we have not sinned, we are calling God a liar and showing that His word has no place in our hearts.

It's time to pull our heads out of the sand! These are things we make excuses for so that we can continue in our sin without feeling guilty! We need to stop making excuses! It's time to have a heart-to-heart with God! I know that for most of you, your excuse is that you are only hurting yourself! So why does it matter? Not only do all those things affect every single person who loves you dearly! But your body is not your own! Your body is a temple in which the Holy Spirit dwells. Your body is a vessel to be used for the glory of God!

So what does that tell you about sins that are punishable by man's law? 1 John 3:15 says, "Anyone who hates another brother and sister is really a murderer at heart. And you know that murderers don't have eternal life within them."

You don't even have to commit murder to be a murderer in God's eyes! All you have to do is hate someone!

So what's the good news in all of this?

Jesus died on the cross for all of our sins! Back to 1 John 1:9: "But if we confess our sins to Him, He is faithful and just to forgive us our sins and to cleanse us from all wickedness."

Jesus will forgive us, so that when we meet our Heavenly Father, our slate will be wiped clean!

Praise Jesus!

13

DAY

Have you noticed how quickly people get angry these days? You see people yelling at cashiers, waiters, or waitresses for making minor mistakes. Instead of politely telling people, "Excuse me," people shove their way through, not caring who they trample. I think this has a lot to do with how selfish we have become! Because as long as we are getting what we want and getting to where we need to be, then who cares about what happens to anyone else? Sadly, the more we depend on ourselves instead of God, the worse this is going to become. We will no longer care if every person that we shove or berate is also a son or daughter to someone—the same as you! That person is a brother or sister to someone—the same as you! That person may have a child waiting at home, depending on them! That person may already be suffering from mental health issues, and you just sent them into a downward spiral! Would you want to be responsible for orphaning a child? Just get a free drink? Or to get to your destination a minute sooner? But above all these things, did you realize that this person is also a child of God? THE SAME AS YOU!

2 Timothy 3:2–3 says,

> For people will love only themselves and their money. They will be boastful and proud, scoffing at God, disobedient to their parents, and ungrateful. They will consider nothing sacred. They will be unloving and unforgiving; they will slander others and have no self-control. They will be cruel and hate what is good.

The other side of this is the cruel part, which is that some people just want to be mean. Whatever is tormenting them in life, they release that torment onto other people instead of giving it to Jesus.

Matthew 5:21–22 says,

> You have heard that our ancestors were told, "You must not murder. If you commit murder, you are subject to judgement. But I say, if you are even angry with someone, you are subject to judgement! If you call someone an idiot, you are in danger of being brought before the court. And if you curse someone, you are in danger of the fires of hell."

Is your anger toward someone you don't even know and who you will most likely never see again appropriate? All because they forgot to put "no tomatoes" on your order? Or something that can easily be fixed? So tell me! Is getting angry worthy of the judgment you would face?

For those who we are so quick to get angry with or lash out at, remember that they are not robots—they are humans! They make mistakes! Just as you do. They are also the BELOVED children of God Almighty! Just as you are!

14

DAY

How many of you know someone who is beyond stubborn? Who denies that there is a God? Someone who won't even have a discussion about God?

We have discussed before that the only way to get into heaven is through Jesus Christ! He is the only one who can save your soul.

Romans 14:11 says, "For the scriptures say, 'As surely as I live, says the Lord, every knee will bend to me, and every tongue will declare allegiance to God.'"

Now I may be a little bit of an instigator because I enjoy telling those stubborn nonbelievers that verse. Dude! No matter what you do or say! YOU WILL KNEEL DOWN IN FRONT OF GOD AND DECLARE HIM GOD! You will have to tell Him to His face why you defiled His name your whole life! You will have to tell Him to His face why you chose to worship anything else but Him! There will be no choice here. There will be no pleading for the fifth.

I had one person tell me that they would get saved then. Folks, when you kneel down in front of God Almighty, giving Him an account of your life, that means you have left this life and moved on into eternity. Your fate will have already been sealed by that point. Your time for making your own personal choice is over; you made your choice. Jesus won't know your name. Therefore, He won't be able to introduce you to His Father as His brother or sister.

Matthew 10:32–33 says, "Everyone who acknowledges me publicly here on earth, I will also acknowledge before my Father in Heaven. But everyone who denies me here on earth, I will also deny before my Father in Heaven."

These stubborn folks will be begging and pleading for forgiveness. The reality of hell will have set in. And it is not, in fact, a hotel party! There is no alcohol! No drugs! No strobe lights!

Oh, how easily they can avoid this embarrassment! Surrender to God now! As people who have already surrendered, it is our job to tell everyone what we can about our awesome Lord! We are to tell them about the freedom we have received! And that they can be free as well. That the awesome power of Jesus Christ, His Father, and the Holy Spirit is waiting for them at their fingertips! It is our job to share what we have found!

Mark 16:15 says, "And He told them, 'Go into all the world and preach the Good News to everyone.'"

No matter what people may say, what is the worst that could happen? The worst that could happen is that you planted a seed in them! You put something in them that they will have to think about and contemplate! The Holy Spirit loves to water those seeds! Then it's fun to watch those seeds sprout, especially in cases we might think would be the most unlikely!

Don't underestimate God!
He is mighty and glorious!
And He is for each one of us!

15
DAY

Who do you trust the most in your life? Your parents? Siblings? Spouse? How many of those people have broken your trust and then had to rebuild that area of your relationship? People will always fail you! Just as you will fail many people! We are all humans, and each one of us will make mistakes!

How much do you trust Jesus? Imagine with me for a moment that the president gets the crazy idea that every person in America has to bow down and worship him and only him. That we were to only pray to him, and if you were caught worshiping any other thing, any other god, or God Himself, you would be executed in front of the whole town.

(This may be a little old school, but it is not out of reach for what may happen in the future!) What would you do? Would you trust God to protect you? Or would you break God's trust in you and betray Him?

Daniel wouldn't betray his Lord and Savior! He refused to bow down to King Darius! King Darius loved Daniel! But he could not change the law for thirty days! Daniel 6:16–17 says,

> So at last the king gave orders for Daniel to be arrested and thrown into the den of lions. The king said to him, "May your God, whom you serve so faithfully, rescue you." A stone was brought and placed over the mouth of the den. The king sealed the stone with his own royal seal

and the seals of his nobles, so that no one could rescue Daniel.

What would you do? Would you crack? Would you remember that this life is just a blink compared to eternity? Would you allow yourself to be a martyr for the Lord?

Daniel 6:19–23 continues,

> Very early the next morning, the king got up and hurried out to the lion's den. When he got there, he called out in anguish, "Daniel, servant of the living God! Was your God, whom you serve so faithfully able to rescue you from the lions?" Daniel answered, "Long live the King! My God sent His angels to shut the lion's mouths so that they would not hurt me, for I have been found innocent in His sight. And I have not wronged you, your majesty."

Would you trust God to send His angels to hold the mouths of the lions shut so that you could snuggle with them and get a good night's sleep? Daniel said, "I have not wronged you." We are to be respectful of those in power. We are to help them and serve them to the best of our ability! But we are never to bow down and worship them. Or expect them to hear and answer our prayers.

Heaven will be our reward! Whether it comes early or late in our lives. Do not betray the King of Kings and Lord of Lords!

Once King Darius got Daniel out of the den, he sent a message to the entire kingdom. Daniel 6:26–27 says,

> I decree that everyone throughout my kingdom should tremble with fear before the God of Daniel, for He is the living God, and He will endure forever. His kingdom will never be destroyed, and His rule will never end. He rescues and saves His people; He performs mirac-

ulous signs and wonders in the Heavens and on earth. He has rescued Daniel from the power of the lions.

How cool would that be to get a letter from the White House that stated:

> On April 5, 2023, we attempted to execute John Smith on the front lawn of the White House. Every bullet fired went around his head. His mighty God saved him! You all should think about praising his God instead!

16
DAY

When the devil attacks, our first response is typically "Why, God! Why would you let this happen to me? It's just not fair! It's not right! I don't like it!" Sometimes it's easier to just get mad at God. That's okay! As long as you don't stay mad at God! He is right there with you! Asking, "Do you trust ME? Are you willing to let Me help you? Are you willing to walk with Me?"

Job's story is a great one to look at when talking about when things get rough and how to handle them. Please bear with me; this may end up being broken up into a few parts.

Job Chapter 10 started Job's plea to God about his awful life:

> I am disgusted with my life. Let me complain freely. My bitter soul must complain. I will say to God, "Don't simply condemn me—tell me the charge you are bringing against me. Are your eyes like those of a human? Do you see things only as people see them? Is your lifetime only as long as ours? Is your life so short that you must quickly probe for my guilt and search for my sin? Although you know I am not guilty, no one can rescue me from your hands." (Job 10:1–7)

You see, Job had everything—a wife, kids, and a thriving farm! He had camels, cows, and donkeys! He was a man of integrity, and he loved God! Then one day, while Satan still had access to heaven, he started his shenanigans on Job. He wanted to test Job's true loyalty to God. So Satan went to God and asked if he could test him. God said yes, but that he couldn't harm him physically in any way. So Satan, being the worm that he is, killed off all of Job's animals—every single one of them! Then Job found out that all of his farmhands had died! And just to top it off, he got word that all of his children died in a tragic accident where his son's house caved in. All of his children were in that house for dinner.

I think this would bring anyone to a pretty rough spot. Job, to say the least, was utterly distraught and racked with grief, but through all of that, he stayed faithful to God. So that made Satan push further. The Lord told Satan, "Don't take his life." So Satan gave Job boils from head to toe.

This is when Job started to cry out. He wrote many letters to many people, crying out for help. We are going to focus on the one that Job wrote directly to God.

Continuing in Job chapter 10:

> You formed me with your hands; you made me, yet now you completely destroy me. Remember that you made me from dust—will you return me back to dust so soon? You guided my conception and formed me in the womb. You clothed me with skin and flesh, and you knit my bones and sinews together. You gave me life and showed me your unfailing love. My life was preserved by your care. Yet your real motive—your true intent—was to watch me, and if I sinned you would not forgive my guilt. If I am guilty, too bad for me; and even if I am innocent, I can't hold my head high, because I am filled with misery. And if I hold my head high, you hunt me like lion and display your growing anger on me and bring fresh armies on me. Why then, did you deliver me from my mother's womb? why didn't you let me die at birth? It would be as though I

had never existed, going directly from the womb to the grave. I have only a few days left, so leave me alone, that I may have a moment of comfort before I leave—never to return—for the land of darkness and utter gloom. It is a land as dark as midnight, a land of gloom and confusion, where even the light is dark as midnight. (Job 10:8–22)

I know that was long, but I think we can all relate! We don't want to just say, "Hey, this stinks!" We want to cry and whine to anyone who will listen and comfort us! Job breaks it all the way down: "Why did you even create me? Why did you even let me live at birth? If this was what was intended for me! Why?" Job pleads for God to take it all back and pretend like he was never there—undo his birth, uncreate him.

17
DAY

Job's three good friends—Eliphaz, Bildad, and Zophar—came to help Job in his time of misery. When they arrived, Job started ranting (rightfully so). His rantings and his friends' responses went on for thirty-seven chapters. Job was just pouring his heart out to anyone who would listen, looking for answers as to why this was happening and naturally wanting to know what he did wrong! Why did he deserve this?

The Lord started to reply in Chapter 38. So here we go:

> Then the Lord answered Job from the whirlwind: "Who is this that questions my wisdom with such ignorant words? Brace yourself like a man, because I have some questions for you, and you must answer them. Where were you when I laid the foundations of the earth? Tell me, if you know so much. Who determines its dimensions and stretched out the surveying line? What supports its foundations, and who laid its cornerstone as the morning stars sang together and all the angels shouted for joy?" (Job 38:1–7)

The Lord continued on and on about everything that He created and everything that happened on a day-to-day basis, and He assured Job that He controlled it all. God raised the sun! God made the sun go down! So who is to question God? To be so bold to call God out! God continued with:

> Can you shout to the clouds and make it rain? Can you make lightning appear and cause it to strike as you direct? who gives intuition to the heart and instinct to the mind? Who is wise enough to count all the clouds? Who can tilt the water jars of Heaven when parched ground is dry and the soil has hardened into clods? (Job 38:34–38)

God was asking Job if he too was capable of doing what God does. God continued through chapter 39, asking Job so many questions. And then in chapter 40, the tone of the questions starts to change:

> Then the Lord said to Job, "Do you still want to argue with the Almighty? You are God's critic, but do you have the answers?" Then Job replied to the Lord, "I am nothing, how could I ever find the answers? I will cover my mouth with my hand. I have said too much already, I have nothing more to say." (Job 40:1–5)

Then the Lord continues on asking questions and telling Job about all the things He created and how He placed them specifically to their needs so they could thrive! So in Job 42:2, it says, "I know that you can do anything, and no one can stop you."

Through everything, Job stayed loyal to God! He might have asked hard questions! But he never bashed God or talked poorly of Him! However, two of the friends that Job ranted to did not stay loyal. Their responses were harsh toward God. Then God went to them. God commanded them to go to Job with a burnt offering for themselves and then to have Job pray for them. When Job did pray for them, he was rewarded for staying loyal and faithful through his entire trial. God restored everything he once had, plus so much more!

Sometimes, the sneaky, creepy little devil attacks. During those attacks, God is paying extra attention to how we react! He wants to see if we will stay loyal to Him—that we will seek Him during those attacks! And when we come out on the other side, God is always sure to bless us! Just as we are to be sure to praise Him!

Folks! God is good! Will you let Him show you how good He is?

DAY 18

Is it enough to say, "I believe in Jesus"? If asked, you surely would never deny Jesus Christ! But what does that mean to you? Does that mean you believe you are going to heaven if you drop dead right now?

Have you ever asked Jesus to be your Lord and Savior? Have you asked Jesus to forgive your sins? Have you knelt down at the altar or at the foot of your bed and cried out to Jesus and told Him just how much you need Him in your life?

How certain are you that if you found yourself at the feet of the throne right now, Jesus would call you "brother or sister" and introduce you to His Father God?

Matthew 10:32–33 says, "Everyone who acknowledges me publicly here on earth, I will also acknowledge before my Father in Heaven. But everyone who denies me here on earth, I will also deny before my Father in Heaven."

Okay! Great! You've got that down. It would be really humbling for you to go to heaven and hear Jesus say to the Father that He does not know you!

So is your declaration of belief enough? What is enough? Does anyone know what enough means in the eyes of God?

John 14:6 says, "Jesus told him, 'I am the way, the truth, and the life. No one can come to the Father except through me.'"

So I can tell you that it is your starting place! You have to have a relationship with Jesus! He is the only way, the truth, and the life! I am talking about a deep relationship. Jesus should be your number 1 confidant! He is the one you tell all your deep, dark secrets! He is the one you should be asking for advice from. You should be crying on His shoulder for the things that break your heart.

Jesus did not die on the cross to save your life, so you could believe in Him like He was equal to the Easter Bunny or Santa Claus. If your thoughts and feelings are equal to your thoughts and beliefs about the Easter Bunny and Santa Claus, my one and only suggestion to you would be to get on your knees and start talking to Jesus. He will reveal Himself to you. He will show you just how real He really is!

Let Psalm 18:1–3 be your prayer and be your praise: "I love you Lord; you are my strength. The Lord is my rock, my fortress, and my savior; He is my shield, the power that saves me. I called on the Lord, who is worthy of praise, and He saved me from my enemies."

I urge you to read the rest of that chapter! Jesus wants to save you! He wants to pull you out of your mess! Will you let Him?

19

DAY

What are the five most important things in your life? If you were told that you were going to a remote island, what are the five things you would put up a fight to take with you? I can imagine children being at the top of most lists! Maybe pets? Spouse?

Think about this verse while thinking about the above questions: Matthew 10:37–39 says,

> If you love your father or mother more than you love me, you are not worthy of being mine; or if you love your son or daughter more than me, you are not worthy of being mine. If you refuse to take up your cross and follow me, you are not worthy of being mine. If you cling to your life, you will lose it; but if you give up your life for me, you will find it.

Wow! For just three verses, there is a whole lot packed in there! So go back to that first question. How many of you had God, Jesus, or the Bible in your top five? I think we have work to do.

God is our true Father. He is our Creator. It's the same for our mothers and fathers; God is their true Father. He is their Creator, too. He is to be loved and praised first. He is to be our example. We can love and respect our earthly parents, but they are humans too. They will fail us at some point. That's a guarantee. God, the Father, is perfect and perfectly loving. We are to put nothing above Him, including mommy and daddy.

Then it goes on to talk about our sons and daughters! Many of you are probably thinking, "But they are my flesh and blood!" Yes, BUT they are God's CREATIONS—a miracle that He is loaning to you! He is trusting you to teach them about His love. We are to be thankful for His gift of our beautiful children and praise Him for them.

Have you ever heard of the term "agape love"? Well, God loves us with agape love. It's a type of love that we will never understand while we are here on earth. It's a marvelous love, so strong, bold, and real. It's a type of love you could never imagine. God loves each one of us with such fierceness and unapologetically. He sent HIS ONLY Son to die for us!

Let me ask you this: Would you send your one and only son to go through what Jesus went through? Could you allow that to happen if it was going to save one person? Ten people? One hundred people? One thousand people? An entire nation? Would a number matter? I find it hard to fathom! God's love for us is so wondrous! It's indescribable! He does so much for us! Is it too much to ask that our Creator, Savior, and loving Father be put at the top of our top five?

20
DAY

Matthew 10:37–39 says,

> If you love you father and mother more than you love me, you are not worthy of being mine; or if you love you son or daughter more than me; you are not worthy of being mine. If you refuse to take up your cross and follow me, you are not worthy of being mine. If you cling to your life, you will lose it; but if you give up your life for me, you will find it.

So we talked about loving God above all else, above our mothers, fathers, sons, and daughters. But what does it mean for us to pick up our own crosses? We have crosses? Where? Huh?

Well, thanks to Adam and Eve for eating that delicious apple, from which they were strictly prohibited! Because of them, we are all lucky enough to inherit their sinful nature. That is why Jesus HAD to die on the cross for our sins. He's the only one who could. He's the only one who has lived a sinless life. He paid the price for us.

So when it's said, "Take up your cross and follow me," Jesus is saying, "What sins do you struggle with? What things do you need to lay at my feet? Will you cry to me for help?" We each have specific sins that we deal with. For many, it's an addiction. Addiction doesn't end with drugs and alcohol. It's drugs, alcohol, gambling, food, sex, porn, etc. For a few, it's murder. As we know, there are many areas of sin! But Jesus is saying, "I see your struggle! Pick up that habit (that cross) and walk with me. As long as you are walking with me, I will help you stay clear of those urges. I will help you overcome those deep, dark emotions."

Then the last part says, "Cling to your life and you will lose it. But if you live for me, you will find it."

We have discussed this before: If you treasure yourself the most or live the best life you can for your own happiness, then you will find eternal death. But if you live your life for the Father, you will put Him first in everything. Then you will find life! Not just on earth, but an eternal life in heaven. God never promised an easy life here on earth. In fact, He said quite the opposite. He did promise that if we trusted Him with everything that we were, He would take care of us and reward us with an eternity in heaven.

2 Corinthians 5:10 says, "For we must all stand before Christ to be judged. We will each receive whatever we deserve for the good or evil we have done in this earthly body."

21
DAY

Each one of us was created for a reason—our very own purpose and destiny. For some of us, our paths may never cross! But that doesn't mean that something you do will never impact me in any way, or vice versa. Every action has a reaction, but did you ever think about the fact that a reaction is also an action? So now every reaction also has a reaction. Which is why when one person makes a silly mistake, it could affect people they will never meet in their lifetimes.

Let's say I am driving down a dark country road and your dog runs out into the street. I hit the poor pup, and he passes away. I may never meet you in my lifetime, but I just broke your heart and accidentally took your beloved pup from you!

But God made each one of us special and unique and gave each of us a mission on earth. Mark 16:15 says, "Go into all the world and preach the Good News to everyone."

But some of us are quiet, and some are shy. Some people stutter and are embarrassed. That's OKAY! That means some of us were made to yell from the pulpit. Some of us were made to rock babies while singing, "Jesus Loves You." Some of us were made for writing, studying, setting up, or building churches. We each have a role to play!

1 Corinthians 12:18–26 says,

> But our bodies have many parts, and God has put each part just where he wants it. How strange a body would be if it only had one part! Yes, there are many parts, but only one body.

> The eye can never say to the hand, "I don't need you." The head can't say to the feet, "I don't need you." In fact, some parts of the body that seem weakest and least important are actually the most necessary. And the part we regard as less honorable are those we clothe with the greatest care. So we carefully protect those parts that should not be seen. While the more honorable parts do not require the special care. So God has put the body together such that extra honor and care given to those parts that have less dignity. This makes for harmony among the members, so that all the members care for each other. If one part suffers, all the parts suffer with it, and if one part is honored, all the parts are glad.

I have just recently started to learn my role, and let me tell you, God can switch it up at any time. Always ensure that as you step into roles, the Lord is directing you. Trust me, you will get confirmations in the oddest ways sometimes. Some will make you belly laugh out loud! Ensure that you thank God for each assurance that He gives you! If it is not God speaking but the enemy just being his pesky distracting self, you won't receive those confirmations from Him. Ensure that you are seeking and listening to the Lord.

When I was a child, I was very shy. I would hide behind my dad when meeting anyone new. I was also that child who, as soon as you got me to smile or speak to you, was all in! You were my instant best friend! I was loud. I spoke loudly; I laughed loudly. I was exuberantly happy to see you. And every time we came into contact, my greetings were filled with giant bear hugs and laughter. Unfortunately, every time, it was followed up with being told to knock it off. That no one appreciated my energy. I was to be quiet. It didn't take long for that sparkle to fade and for me to be quiet.

I didn't understand the balance. I was like a puppy. Even after the obnoxious greeting, I was still craving and pawing for more attention, like an oversized lap dog. After being told by multiple people to not act that way and to stop, I did just that—I stopped.

It wasn't until recently that multiple people came to me (some I had never met before) with a word from God for me. (When you get the same word multiple times, LISTEN TO IT!) I was told to let go of whatever was silencing me! Wow! I never thought about that. I also didn't realize how timid I had actually become!

I was created to be bold! I was created to be a little extra! I was created to be loud! I was created to have thunderous belly laughs! That is who I am! Most importantly, that is who I am in Christ! I have embraced it, and I am no longer embarrassed by who I am!

God saved this timid soul. He made me bold enough to send out these tough questions to make y'all think. Seek the Lord for your purpose!

22
DAY

How many of you have watched every season of *American Idol*? How about *America's Got Talent*? *The Voice*? *The Bachelor*? *The Bachelorette*? *Bachelor in Paradise*? *Tough as Nails*? The list goes on. All these shows have multiple things in common. All of these people are coming on a show to showcase themselves, whether through talent, beauty, or strength. At the same time, every single one of them is searching for something they cannot find there. Many are searching for fame, acceptance, or a place to call home. I even considered, at one point, trying out for *American Idol* when I was in high school. (I might've made it to the bloopers.)

I find it funny how the different stages of our lives shape what is at the top of our list of things we desire to search out. First-time parents want to be the best parents. When starting a new job, you just want to be the best employee. But when Jesus is above all of that, everything else always falls into place.

In 1 Thessalonians 1:8–10, it says,

> And now the word of the Lord is ringing out from you to people everywhere, even beyond Macedonia and Achaia, for wherever we go we find people telling us about your faith in God. We don't need to tell them about it. For they keep talking about the wonderful welcome you gave us and how you turned away from idols to serve the living and true God. And they speak of how you are looking forward to the coming of God's Son

from Heaven—Jesus, whom God raised from the dead. He is the one who has rescued us from the terrors of the coming judgement.

This is what I would love for my legacy to look like. Folks just talking about how I loved them with the love of Jesus and how I shared and taught them about that love with all of my being. I would want that, not just for the people at the store or at the bank, but for my kids and everyone in my life.

I had a family member who passed away many years ago. We had to cut the line at the visitation to start the funeral. This person touched everyone they talked to. Even the person who bagged their groceries at the local store showed up in tears. The funny thing is, I didn't know this person who died the same way everyone else did. I never even thought this person liked me. I remembered sitting at the funeral, wishing that I knew the person everyone around me was mourning. I felt out of place, like I had shown up to the wrong funeral.

I don't want a single soul to feel that way about me when I go home to heaven. Romans 14:13 says, "So let's stop condemning each other. Decide instead to live in such a way that you will not cause another believer to stumble and fall."

I try to always make a brave attempt to resolve conflicts that come my way quickly. Sometimes, those conflicts have helped create boundaries that I needed to set up to protect myself from future incidents. But I would never want my anger to cause another person to stumble in their faith, or maybe sobriety, or maybe even depression, but most of all in their walk with the Lord.

DAY 23

What does family mean to you? This little word "family" is one of the most complicated words I have ever come across! Everyone has a different perception of its meaning. Yes, we were all born because a man loved a woman, whether it was for a moment, a lifetime, or maybe even a donation. A woman gives birth to a child. But then everything goes out of the window from this moment on because there is no "normal." Not every man sticks around. Not every woman keeps a child. Not everyone who keeps their child should keep their child. Some children grow up having weekly "family" dinners with aunts, uncles, cousins, and grandparents—with all those family members highly involved in their lives. Some children grow up lonely, with none of those people in their lives.

One thing that is built into each of us is the need to be loved and to feel accepted and wanted. Children who grow up in non-loving and/or abusive homes typically go searching for the love they OH-SO-desire. More often than not, they find that acceptance within a gang. They find that "love" through prostitution. I put quotes around that love, because that is not true love.

God implanted in us the need for love and acceptance! But that need, want, or desire cannot be fulfilled by earthly things or people. It can only be fulfilled by Jesus Christ!

Ephesians 2:19–21 says,

> So now you gentiles are no longer strangers and foreigners. You are citizens along with all

of God's holy people. You are members of God's family. Together, we are His house, built on the foundation of the apostles and the prophets. And the cornerstone is Christ Jesus Himself. We are carefully joined together in Him, becoming a Holy temple for the Lord.

I LOVE THAT! We are citizens of God's holy people! When you surround yourself with godly people and create lasting relationships with them, it will be the best investment you could make in your life! For it is our godly brothers and sisters who we love and make our family! They are the ones who will still be your friends in heaven! They will be the ones you do "life" with—that is, eternal life. 1 John 3:1 says, "See how very much our Father loves us, for He calls us His children, and that is what we are! But the people who belong to this world don't recognize that we are God's children because they don't know Him." (YET)

I like to add YET to statements like that because there is hope for everyone! There is room for every person on this earth to repent and turn to God!

I once knew someone who lived a brokenhearted life. His parents couldn't care for him, so he was given up for adoption. He was adopted into a loving Christian home. He was raised in church but decided to live in desperation because his parents didn't want him. (Folks, when someone gives up a baby for adoption, it is not because they don't want the child. They go through heartbreak and torment over their decision, and then wonder daily if they made the right one.) He lived in desperation because he didn't know his biological dad. When he finally found his dad, it was too late to meet him; he had passed away. The man I knew drowned the pain with any substance he could and drank every moment he was awake. He lived in torment.

He never let God heal those wounds. He never let Jesus welcome him into the family that he OH so craved and that his heart cried out for.

Folks, I tell you this because it's time to give up your earthly family heartbreaks. (I am not saying to give up your earthly family!) However, it is time to let the Holy Spirit heal your hearts and your minds.

Psalms 147:3 says, "He heals the broken hearted and bandages their wounds."

24

DAY

What do you do when your heart is breaking? I'll admit, I have not had any great tragic losses in my life. My great-grandparents were well into their '80s and '90s when they passed. My grandpa's death was shocking. He was young, and watching his mother bury her son was the hardest part. When my dad passed just a little while ago, it was after watching him suffer for four years. Seeing my grandma, who had already buried her husband and now her third child, was what truly broke my heart. She then passed shortly after my dad.

What do you do in those moments of grief when nothing makes sense? You don't know if you should laugh at all the good times or continue to cry for what could have been!

It wasn't until recently in my life that I realized that grief comes from different things, not just from losing a loved one. Sometimes, it's the grief of a failed relationship, the grief of losing a job and having to start over, or the grief of having to move on and leave behind memories. Grieving looks different for everyone, and everyone grieves things differently! Some people think it's silly to grieve the loss of a life! Some people grieve everything.

Matthew 5:4 says, "God blesses those who mourn, for they will be comforted."

Psalms 147:3 says, "He heals the broken hearted and bandages their wounds."

God will comfort you during your season of mourning! But He doesn't want you to stay there! He doesn't want life-changing events to actually change your entire life! Sometimes, it's hard to hear the words "move on." But the fact is that you cannot stay put.

Lamentations 3:17–18 says, "Peace has been stripped away, and I have forgotten what prosperity is. I cry out, 'my splendor is gone! Everything I had hoped for from the Lord is lost!'" (This man had clearly given up.)

"The thought of my suffering and homelessness is bitter beyond words, I will never forget this awful time, as I grieve over my loss" (Lamentations 3:19–20). (Yes, we will always have our memories.)

"Yet I still dare to hope when I remember this: The faithful love of the Lord never ends! His mercies never cease. Great is His faithfulness; His mercies begin afresh each morning; I say to myself, 'The Lord is my inheritance; therefore, I will hope in Him!'" (Lamentations 3:21–24).

God wants you to have hope in Him! Let things stink for a moment. Sit with your feelings for a moment, but don't stay there! Get up! Take one tiny step at a time if you have to. Just make sure that the tiny step is forward and not backward!

25
DAY

"Blessed are those who wash their robes. They will be permitted to enter through the gates of the city and eat the fruit from the tree of life. Outside the city are the dogs—the sorcerers, the sexually immoral, the murderers, the idol worshipers, and all who love to lie" (Revelations 22:14–15).

Which one are you? Are you inside the gates? Feasting on the tree of life? Or are you outside, wishing you were inside? Or are you outside, completely living happily in all the lies you have grown to believe?

I was outside for a long time, looking like a puppy wanting to go home. I allowed the lies to drag me further and further away for a very long time. Let's be real—sinning is fun. As long as you're in it, it's fun. Imagining a life without "fun" can be daunting! However, when you find the true joy in the Lord! And His full embrace, you will know just how empty that "fun" really was.

My "fun" led me down a very dark and twisted path, as most "fun" (sin) does. Until eventually, you hit this bottom—some people call it rock bottom—but I don't remember rocks being down there. It was lonely, dark, and scary.

But you know what? Jesus was sitting there next to me the entire time! That whole time, He was crying out to me to come home! He sat there begging and pleading with me to just take His hand! And to just trust Him! It's funny how stubborn we can be! I know He was screaming in my face for a long time, but it took that long for me to hear it.

On our journeys, it usually takes a breaking point where we say, "I just can't do this anymore! I just can't handle this on my own!" This is when we start to hear Him crying out for us.

If only we could start by listening before we get to that point! But here is what I can tell you: When you find that peace in the Lord and you learn to put your trust in Him, you will never find yourself in that dark, scary, isolated pit again!

John 16:31–33 says,

> Jesus asked, "Do you finally believe? But the time is coming—indeed it's here now—when you will be scattered, each one going his own way, leaving Me alone. Yet I am not alone because the Father is with Me. I have told you all this so that you may have peace in Me. Here on earth you will have many trials and sorrows. But take heart, because I have overcome the world."

God didn't promise us an easy life! But He did promise to be faithful! Put your trust in Him! You will feel the difference! Start eating from the tree of life! Come into His city.

26
DAY

Isaiah 44:22 says, "I have swept away sins like a cloud. I have scattered your offenses like the morning mist. Oh, return to me, for I have paid the price to set you free."

God is crying out for you! When God says, OH, or we say OH to God, it is our deepest desires coming out. "OH, return to me." He's yelling! Crying out! And pleading for you to listen. Quit running! Start running to the Father!

> This is what the Lord says—your Redeemer and Creator, "I am the Lord, who made all things. I alone stretched out the Heavens. Who was with me when I made the earth?" (Isaiah 44:24)

There is no one before God. He is the Creator of all time, of all things, and of all universes.

> I expose the false prophet as liars and make fools of fortune tellers. I cause the wise to give bad advice, this proving them to be fools. (Isaiah 44:25)

God is going to expose those who lift themselves up on pedestals! He is going to expose those who want to be praised, lifted up, or idolized in any way. He's going to make those who claim to know things that they cannot know look like fools! I don't know about you, but I don't want to be a part of either one of those categories!

God is crying out for you to bow to Him and ask for forgiveness! Repent of your sins. Repent for wanting to be idolized! Repent for wanting to be equal to or greater than the one and only God Almighty!

As you look around your town, state, or country, you see how things are getting out of hand at a rapid pace. Everyone is being silenced, and evil is wreaking havoc. Did you know that ending these troubles starts with you? It starts with us falling to our knees and begging for forgiveness in the same way God is begging us to come to Him. By starting our lives over for the Lord, we become an example for others to follow! Psalms 107:2 says, "Has the Lord redeemed you? Then speak out! Tell others he has redeemed you from your enemies."

So speak out. Tell your story! The more people who come home to the Lord, the greater the opportunity to take away the devil's playground! Let us keep pushing the devil further into the desert! Give him no room in our country!

Listen to the words of God: "Oh, return to me."

Let our response be, "Oh, Lord, forgive me!"

27
DAY

What does repentance mean to you? I think some of the most important words in the Bible have received different meanings. Some that cause people to shy away from them or refuse to understand more. For instance, I always associated repentance with meeting with a priest and being assigned a number of Hail Marys. The odd thing is, I have only been to a Catholic church once in my whole life! Now I am NOT bashing Catholics! Don't twist my words! I am saying that I thought only Catholics had to repent! HA—how silly I was! They may repent differently from other denominations, and perhaps they put more emphasis on repentance! But truly, every denomination that is serving the one true God should put that much emphasis on repentance! Sure, we talk about forgiveness, and while repentance and forgiveness go hand in hand, they are in fact different! So let's dive deeper into that difference!

We have spoken about forgiveness a lot. It's safe to say that we understand that if you do something dumb (i.e., yell at someone, have angry thoughts, etc.), we can say, "Lord, forgive me."

Repentance is a little deeper. The dictionary describes it as sincere regret or remorse. Think of how you would feel as a spouse if you stepped out of your marriage. In that moment when you realize you have committed the ultimate betrayal against your spouse, wouldn't you beg and plead with your spouse to forgive you? Wouldn't you cry out to them how truly sorry you are? This is repentance. It is when you are on your knees, begging and pleading with God to forgive you and to change you so that you don't do that offensive thing again.

Psalms 130:1–2 says, "From the depths of despair, O Lord, I call for your help. Hear my cry, O Lord. Pay attention to my prayer."

Do you see the desperation? They say, "Hear my cry, O Lord!"

Psalms 130:3–4 says, "Lord, if you kept a record of our sins, who O Lord could ever survive? But you offer forgiveness, that we might learn to fear you."

Praise God for forgiveness! We don't have to walk around in shame and guilt!

Acts 3:19–20 says, "Now repent of your sins and turn to God, so that your sins may be wiped away. Then times of refreshment will come from the presence of the Lord, and He will again send you Jesus, your appointed Messiah."

Wow! Just like that, God can refresh your spirit, your heart, and your soul! Just like that, God will wipe away your sin. Just like that, Jesus is at your fingertips again—to teach us and help us grow. Simply amazing.

What do you need to repent of? What is the Holy Spirit telling you? What guilt do you walk with? What shame are you trying to hide? Are you listening for the Holy Spirit to reveal to you what the answers are?

28
DAY

Do you need freedom? What do you need freedom from? An abusive relationship? From drugs? From childhood trauma? Freedom can look like many different things! And freedom is unique for each one of us, but one thing that is very true is that each one of us needs freedom from something!

Galatians 5:13–14 says, "For you have been called to live in freedom, my brothers and sisters. But don't use your freedom to satisfy your sinful nature. Instead, use your freedom to serve one another in love. For the whole law can be summed up in this one command: 'Love your neighbor as yourself.'"

You often see people (especially in Alcoholics Anonymous) who find their freedom, then become sponsors for people who are searching for their freedom. This is what it means to serve one another in love! We all have things that we have gone through. God wants us to use those moments of heartache to help others get through theirs.

Galatians 5:15 says, "But if you are always biting and devouring one another, watch out! Beware of destroying one another!"

I think of bullies when I read that scripture. Don't be a bully to someone who is obviously in need of love and help (which is every single one of us). Be uplifting and loving to each person you meet!

2 Corinthians 3:16–18 says,

> But whenever someone turns to the Lord, the veil is taken away. For the Lord is the Spirit, and wherever the Spirit of the Lord is, there is freedom. So all of us who have had that veil

removed can see and reflect the glory of the Lord. And the Lord—who is the Spirit—makes us more and more like Him as we are changed into His glorious image.

The Spirit of the Lord removes the "veil," or blinders, from our eyes to make us capable of seeing the areas in which we need help! To see the areas where God desires to bring freedom. These are the stories that you hear from drug addicts. They will be in an abandoned building, curled up in a dark corner, scared, hungry, and wanting their next fix when the Lord comes, removes their "veil," and shows them that they need help.

When the Lord shows up and asks to take your hand or if He can carry you for a while, it is up to you to take His hand! It is up to you to let Him pick you up! It will be your decision to make! It baffles me when people say "no." You have to remember that we all have free will! We can say no. I don't advise it! I advise that you raise your arms up and cling to His neck! Wrap your legs around His waist, lay your head on His shoulders, and rest for a while!

The Lord is offering each one of us freedom! Are you going to take His hand? Are you going to trust Him?

29

DAY

Let's face it, most people, preachers, and teachers don't talk about the cross. The less we talk about things, the further from our minds they become. What do you know about the cross? What do you know about the events leading up to the cross? Do you believe in the cross? Do you believe our Savior died on the cross?

Let me paint a picture for you. Jesus knew what was coming. He begged God, His Father, to find another way! God explained to Him that this was the only way to save the nations—to save generations after generations! A normal person would have run to hide somewhere! But Jesus went willingly! He was arrested! He didn't put up a fight. He was mocked. The soldiers spit on His face. They bashed Him over the head with a stick after putting a crown of thorns on it. (We aren't talking about the thorns on a rose.) These thorns pierced His head and sunk into His skull.

The rest of the story as it was told in Matthew is pretty mild. It's written in a "very matter-of-fact" type of way. But when you go to Isaiah 53:5–7, it says a bit more:

> But He was pierced for our rebellion, crushed for our sins. He was beaten so we could be whole. He was whipped so we could be healed. All of us, like sheep, have strayed away. We have left God's path to follow our own. Yet the Lord laid on Him the sins of us all. He was oppressed and treated harshly, yet He never said a word. He

was led like a lamb to the slaughter. And as sheep is silent before the shearers, He did not open His mouth.

I think those who teach or preach are trying to save us from the utter trauma Jesus went through. They are trying to save us from disturbing mental images. But I think it is important to know exactly the price Jesus paid for us! Some people need the mental image just to have an appreciation of His sacrifice.

So when John was telling his version, he gave a bit more description. He started out like this: "Then Pilate had Jesus flogged with a lead-tipped whip" (John 19:1).

Pilate was a Roman governor, and it was standard practice for the Romans to give thirty-nine lashes when they whipped someone. Now the whip they used on Jesus was a lead-tipped whip! Not a regular whip! Thirty-nine times they slashed through Jesus's back, into His muscles, and then ripped the whip back out of Him. Yes, this is graphic. But this is what Jesus did for you and me! Would you give up your son to go through this? After that brutal beating, Jesus was given to the guards, even though Pilate found Him not guilty. Pilate still handed Him over to the guards.

The Roman guards made Jesus carry His own cross to Golgotha. I can't imagine this being a short walk. With ripped skin and muscles, I just can't imagine. A man named Simon was forced to carry the cross at the last stretch of the walk. I can imagine Jesus was struggling to stand, let alone walk. Once they got to their destination, the cross was laid down, and Jesus was laid on top of it. With His hands outstretched, they nailed them to the cross. One foot over the other—His feet were nailed together into the cross. Then the cross was lifted and dropped into a hole. That force alone had to have ripped through part of His hands.

As He hung there, the weight of His body would start to drown His lungs. He would have to raise Himself up to get good, deep breaths. The guards, getting impatient for Jesus and the other two who were nailed to the crosses to die, asked Pilates if they could speed things up. John 19:32–34 says, "So the soldiers came and broke the legs of the two men crucified with Jesus. But when they came to Jesus, they saw that He was already dead, so they didn't break His legs. One of the soldiers, however, pierced His side with a spear, and immediately blood and water flowed out."

The MAN was DEAD, and they still drained Him of His blood.

People, what happened to Jesus is more gruesome than anyone could ever portray.

John 3:16, the infamous verse, says, "For God so loved the world: He gave His one and only Son, so that everyone who believes in Him will not perish but have eternal life." What will it take for you to be all in?

I sometimes think that because we can't see it or haven't witnessed it, we find it hard to believe. If you had been there, if you had been standing in the crowd, then would you believe?

Question: Do you believe the stories your parents tell you about their past? Do you believe your aunts, uncles, or even grandparents when they speak of events that they personally witnessed? Well, this is Matthew and John's account of what happened. This is their news broadcast!

God literally gave a piece of Himself—His only begotten Son. Jesus was and is the only human to live a holy life, never having committed one sin. He was the only one who could do what He did on the cross that day. In that torment, He took the punishment that you deserve and the punishment that I deserve. He took the punishment for the rapists, the murderers, and the thieves. If Jesus had not done what He did that day, there would not be redemption; there would be no grace!

When will you thank Jesus? When will you be all in? Let Jesus do what He literally died to do—to save you!

DAY 30

At this point, if you have been seriously asking yourself the questions that have been given to you, you should be asking yourself, "What's next?" Do you find yourself yearning for more? Are you being drawn to seek more answers? That is Jesus calling you! He wants you in His family! He wants to tell His Father to prepare a mansion for you as well!

In John 3:3–7, the Bible says this:

> Jesus replied, "I tell you the truth, unless you are born again, you cannot see the Kingdom of God." "What do you mean?" exclaimed Nicodemus. "How can an old man go back into his mother's womb and be born again?" Jesus replied, "I assure you, no one can enter the Kingdom of God without being born of water and the spirit. Humans can reproduce only human life, but the Holy Spirit gives birth to spiritual life. So don't be surprised when I say, you must be born gain."

Many of you are saying, "Huh?" This is going back to John 14:6, where it says, "I am the way, the truth and the life. No one can come to the Father except through me."

This is where salvation comes in.

> If you openly declare that Jesus is Lord and believe in your heart that God raised Him from the dead, you will be saved. (Romans 10:9)

> But how can they call on Him to save them unless they believe in Him? (Romans 10:14)

So where does your belief stand? Are you ready to declare that Jesus Christ is your Lord and Savior? Are you ready to admit that you are a sinner? Are you ready to admit that you need more in your life?

If you are, PRAY! Tell God! Say a prayer of salvation! If you need help, now is a good starting point.

> Dear Lord Jesus, I know that I am a sinner, and I am asking for your forgiveness! I believe you died on the cross for my sins. I believe that God raised you from your grave three days later. Please come into my heart as my Lord and Savior. Help me walk in your footsteps every day.

Pour your heart out to God! He is listening! He is always listening! When you are finished praying, be sure to thank Jesus for His sacrifice! Thank Him for saving you! And thank Him for answering your prayer for salvation!

Sit in the glory of the moment, even if it is just for the moment. Give yourself time to feel God's mercy!

ABOUT THE AUTHOR

Lindsay McMurtry's story is a lot like anyone else's. She is happily living a life for herself! She has worked hard to make her way into the world of management, and even though she works long hours, she loves it. Or so she thinks she does! She has always believed in God! She never denies His existence! But she is not listening to Him! She was not praying! She was not reading her Bible! Until her life flips upside-down in 2020. In the midst of that, God starts working on her. Then one day He asks, "Is your belief enough?" The more she digs into that question, the more God lays it on her heart to share what she finds. She is excited for your journey through this devotional.